DYCE:

a historical miscellany
of an Aberdeenshire Village

C.W. ORD

ISBN: 1-900173-84-0

First published June 2004

Published by
Aberdeen & North-East Scotland Family History Society

Printed by
Rainbow Enterprises, Howe Moss Crescent, Kirkhill Industrial Estate, Dyce, Aberdeen

ACKNOWLEDGEMENTS

Thanks to
the children of Dyce for inspiration;
Sheila Stratton and her family for their knowledge and enthusiasm;
staff at the Local Studies Department at Aberdeen Library
and my family for their help.

CONTENTS

The Parish of Dyce   1
Tumuli; Gouk Stone; Binghill Castle   3
Wells; Landowners; Parkhill   4
The Church; Kirk of St Fergus   5
Bogenjoss Burn   7
Howmoss Circle; Cattle Creep Road; Old Roads   8
The Canal   9
Bridges; The River (unsubstantiated stories)   11
The Turnpike Road; Schools   12
The Meldrum Road   13
Kirkhill Road; Tappies   14
Berry Picking; Lochs   15
William Hay; The Railway   16
Dyce Station; Railway Stations   17
Blacksmiths; The Pondies   18
Daisy Cottage   19
The Mausoleum; Lady's Jointure; Nether Farburn; Mains of Kirkhill   20
Pitmedden; Dyce Quarries   21
St Medan's Church; Saints   22
Lovely Bend; Cothal Mill; Dyce Mills   23
The Holy City; Walking; Band; Drama   24
Shopping; Aberdeen Airport   25
The War Memorial   26
Artist; Writer   27
Minister; Mathematician; Robert Gordon; Lawsons   28
Streets   29
Statistics   30
Poverty; Morality   31
Punishment; Local Stories   32
Memories   33
Index   35
References   37

Photographs at centre pages: Parkhill Lodge; Parkhill Bridge; Dyce Church and Old Kirkyard; Quaker Mausoleum; Liddel Monument; Bishop's Stone; Stone Circle; Canal; Last Fly Boat; Fountain, Station Road; Toll House, Inverurie Road Junction

DYCE

It is uncertain how Dyce got its name. Suggestions are DYCE meaning Southward, or from DICE, the goddess of Justice.

THE PARISH OF DYCE

Dyce has a long history. It was first inhabited 500 to 1000 BC and probably earlier. There is evidence of a later Bronze Age civilisation.

- The Stone Circle at Standingstones, dated 2500 BC, is nearly 60 ft in diameter and consists of eleven upright stones and a big flat stone known as the "altar".

- The Bronze Age Cairn on Marcus Hill which came to light when trees were felled in war time.

- Bronze Age Barrows covering burials or cremations on the higher ground of the parish.

- Urns, containing ashes, found north of Upper Kirkton Farm.

1. Round Cairn at Marcus Hill.

The early people lived mainly around Tyrebagger Ridge, height 823 ft, as the lower ground was mainly moor and swamp. The earliest recorded history is 1316 when Robert the Bruce granted a charter of the Forests of Cordyce to Sir James De Gariouch, the Johnstons of Cookston, for his aid during The Wars of Independence.

Before the railway came to Dyce in the 1860s there was no proper Dyce village. The Parish of Dyce was known as the Meyir (or Muir) of Dyce (Meyir meaning moorland) and was mostly in the Overton and Pitmedden areas where there were many farms and crofts.

Ton (meaning town) was a farm where many people lived and worked, for example Overton, Nether Kirkton and Upper Kirkton. Up to 1865 the village contained two thatched cottages, a carpenter, a shoemaker, a smithy and the Old Inn. Mr Gordon, owner of much of the land gave off feus and more cottages were built. These homes were described as detached cottages with neat front gardens. Dyce became a popular area for businessmen to live. Because of the railway it was very convenient for the town, and Dyce could be reached from the centre of Aberdeen almost as quickly as the west end of Aberdeen could be reached.

2. Kirkton.

To make living in the village more desirable trees were planted and water was supplied from the Overton area. Eventually more water was needed as the number of houses in the area increased.

At the end of the 19th century drainage had been provided to take sewage away from the village and street oil lamps were lit in winter. By this time the village had a post office and shops. A village hall and tennis and bowling greens were planned.

TUMULI

Several small cairns can be traced over the area to the west. These would probably mark the spots where common folk were buried. Often the bodies were cremated. The cairns are of a size, which would equal a cart load of stones.

Part of Cairn Harvey remains west of Dyce Quarry. Another cairn, still fairly complete, stands on part of a ridge known as Slacks Wood near Bendauch Farm. Beside this cairn is a circular hut structure which was built so that its doorway faced south.

GOUK STONE

This prominent stone stands on Bendauch Farm and is visible from the road at Kinaldie. Near it is said to be the Quaich Stone. Tradition has it that the Gouk Stone marks the grave of a general of that name who was killed in battle.

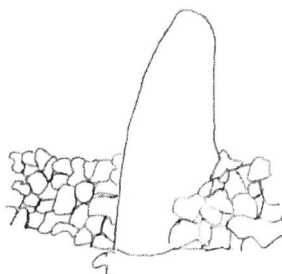

3. Bendauch Stone.

BINGHILL CASTLE

There is a tiny enclosure at the top of the field behind Mountjoy Farm where it is claimed mounds of graves were to be found, while nearby are the massive foundations known as Binghill Castle. Possibly, before the Reformation, a sub-chapel stood in the small enclosure.

WELLS

Pitdourie Well is a strong mineral spring beside the croft of Pitdourie. It was formerly a May-day wishing well. Another spring is known as Johnnie Ririe's Well. He was said to have been a smuggler. The well is now part of the district water supply.

The name Johnnie Ririe is mentioned in the Poll Book 1696. In some instances "Holy Wells" degenerated into "Wishing Wells".

LANDOWNERS

A De Garioch heiress married the first of the Johnstons of Caskieben who held Dyce for centuries until they fell on hard times and had to sell the land.

The next proprietors of the lower ground were the Skenes of Dyce who had a mansion house at Mains of Dyce until 1803. When a bridge was built across the River Don at Parkhill they crossed and built Parkhill House. This was a spacious building, surrounded by trees, with pleasure grounds fronting the Don for about a mile. The original house was built by Skene of Lethenty; the place before that time was known as Glubsgoval.

After the Skenes, the Gordon-Cummings the Gordons of Parkhill were the main landowners of Dyce.

The last of the Gordon family to live at Parkhill was John Gordon. He was an evangelist and set up a mission in Aberdeen. In 1920 Parkhill was sold to Dr Crombie of Crombie Mills who died in the 1930s.

PARKHILL

Various objects of interest lie near at hand. At Parkhill House there stood a Roman Catholic chapel, all of which has vanished except a fragment forming part of the garden wall. In a field to the north is a place known as Cope's Butts, where Sir John Cope exercised his troops on the march against Prince Charlie.

Near Parkhill House is a field where a number of springs rise. The water was collected and brought to the pumping station at Goval and from there turbines forced it to the reservoir nearly two miles away.

Near Parkhill Station, the railway station serving the line to Buchan, a very ancient silver chain was unearthed in 1864 and near the same place a stone cist was found in 1881.

The chain is now a valuable object of interest in a museum in Edinburgh.

THE CHURCH

St Fergus established the first church on the site of the Old Kirkyard and it is not unreasonable to suppose that a church has stood on the spot since then. St Fergus and St Medan were disciples of St Drostan who conducted a mission at Deer towards the end of the 6th century.

In Roman times the church was a vicarage of Kinkell, i.e. the preacher was supplied from Kinkell.

The walls of the Pre-Reformation church still stand in the Old Kirkyard. It was used as the parish church until 1872 when a new church was built near Kirk Cottage. Eventually it was too far distant from the centre of population and was closed in 1926.

The West Church on Pitmedden Road dates from 1869 and to begin with was known as Dyce Free Church. The present church in the village was a mission church which was opened in 1895.The two congregations united in 1936.

KIRK OF ST FERGUS

The original church of St Fergus stood somewhere in the Kirkhill area, as the name would suggest. In the Old Kirkyard are several signs of early times. In the 1300s this church was called The Chapel of St Fergus and belonged to the Knights Templar (a religious order which defended Christian Pilgrims).

The ruins we see in the churchyard are of another old church that was built about 1544 by Alexander Galloway, Rector of Kinkell. The roof was made of heath until approximately 1780.

4. Old Church of St Fergus.

Found in the Kirkyard are the Dyce Symbol Stones. The oldest is a boulder 5ft 6in high marked with "the elephant, the double-disc and Z rod" symbols which date it at about 800AD. There is a 4ft 6in high granite stone with Celtic cross symbols – one of only five such stones known in the area between the River Spey and the River Dee. Three stones varying in size, each with crosses of different design are preserved also. One has been dated to the 8th century. Standing at the doorway is the remains of a stone font and on the inside of the northern wall are the remains of a sacrament house, or aumry, bearing inscriptions. On the skew-put stone on the western gable is an ornamental sheep's head or gargoyle with horns. The image may be linked to the Knights Templar.

In a corner of the kirkyard is the watch house that was built at the time of the grave robbers so that a watch could be kept for those intending to steal bodies of the recently buried.

Peter Brownie, a young farmer from Fintray, and the gravedigger at Newhills (Resurrectionist Marr) used the area as their happy hunting ground. Brownie was never caught but eventually repented and he became a Quaker at Kinmuck. He also designed a mort-safe that was kept in the anatomy department at Aberdeen University. He died in 1886 and is buried in the Quaker Kirkyard at Kinmuck.

In the kirkyard are the rows of graves in memory of the many servicemen of different nationalities killed in the Second World War.

Dyce Parish Church, which stood behind the quarry, replaced the Old Church of St Fergus.

5. Dyce Parish Church.

The Free Church of Dyce was built in 1869 in Pitmedden Road and originally had a tall spire. The spire was taken down in war time for the safety of aircraft using Dyce Airport. At the house beside the church worshippers in the early days could leave their coaches in stables while they went to church. The church has now been demolished and although part of the site is now a parking area the burial ground remains.

6. Dyce Free Church Hall.

At the modern Dyce Parish Church the old church bell can be seen and a marble tablet to the Rev Kemp is set in the north wall. The old bell is lettered "Soli Deo Gloria Michael Burgerhuys MF1642".

An early chapel is believed to have stood at Moss Fetach, the low ground lying between Nether Kirkton and the River Don.

BOGENJOSS BURN

The burn was artificially divided so that both Pitmedden and Standingstones could have parts.

HOWMOSS CIRCLE

It is not certain what the circle of stones represents. Suggestions are: a small fort, a penfold for animals, a hide for bow and arrow hunters or part of a smuggler's still.

CATTLE CREEP ROAD

The cattle creep, which allowed cattle to move from one field to another without straying on the main road, gave its name to the part beyond Woodlands Cottage to the old road north of Marcus Hill.

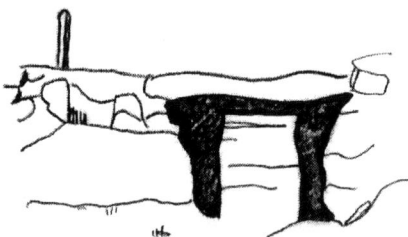

7. Cattle Creep Road

OLD ROADS

Starting from Jollies Howe near Corsehill the road from Aberdeen divided into two: one arm going by the Toll of Tyrebagger to Scotsmill near Begsley with a branch by Blackburn to Kemnay and the other arm going towards Kirkhill then by Bogenjoss Crofts over the hill to Scotsmill then on to Kinellar Kirk. In 1721 it was too costly to maintain these roads between Jollies Howe and Scotsmill so the Bogenjoss route was selected. In 1748 it was changed and the road by the Toll was repaired and used.

The road to Aberdeen was named Via Regia or King's Highway.

Part of the old Dyce road skirted the wall at Parkhill Lodge.

THE CANAL

Dyce was on the Aberdeenshire Canal, constructed 1796-1805, which ran from Aberdeen to Port Elphinstone near Inverurie. The canal was used to move produce to and from the farming areas and the town. Barges were pulled by horses travelling along the tow path. One of the oldest buildings in Dyce was the Old Inn House where the canal passed by and where the barge workers could get refreshments. On the opposite side were stables where the horses were rested and changed. This building was changed to a dwelling house.

The Old Inn was also used by travellers on the road. In 1935 the Inn was pulled down for houses to be built. The two houses, which stand in front of McIntosh Factory stand near the site. Workers laying pipes found the cobbled courtyard of the Old Inn near to the houses.

8. Two views of the Old Inn.

At the coming of the railway the canal was no longer needed. It was drained and railway tracks were laid on some of its path, however some of the outline of the canal and tow path can be seen from the road near to the Gravel Pit and Nether Kirkton Farm. Original canal milestones are still in place at Dyce Parish Church and at Beidleston Farm.

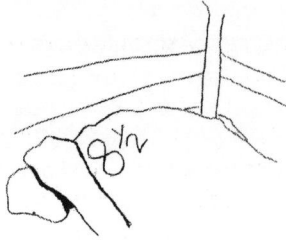

9. Canal 8½ mile stone now placed on a mound near Nether Kirkton where the former Dyce Station stood.

The canal was 18 miles long with 17 locks each about 60ft long. The highest point (168ft above level) was at Lock Cottage, Stoneywood. Depth was 3ft 9in, width 25ft. Goods were carried in covered barges. A man and a boy were the crew and a barge carried about 10 ton of goods. The journey took about 12 hours up or down and freight cost was 1d per ton per mile. Cargoes were such things as coals, lime, manure, oats, potatoes, salt, slates, stone, wood, bones and livestock.

Two iron fly boats carrying 30 to 40 passengers made the double journey daily in two and a half hours. Two or three horses in tandem drew these boats with a boy on the first horse. The fare was 2d a mile, or 2/- fore cabin, 1/6d aft cabin Aberdeen to Inverurie.

People bathed in the canal in summer and skated on it in winter.

Milestones existed at each half mile to fix charges. Horses had jingling bells and boatmen and passengers would shout greetings to people on land as they passed by.

The sign board for the Old Inn, lent by Mr Gordon of Parkhill, was on exhibition at the Dyce stall at a bazaar held in the Music Hall, Aberdeen in 1890. It was believed to be the first attempt of John Phillip, the famous painter, who passed some of his early days in Dyce.

BRIDGES

For centuries there was no bridge across the River Don except for the Brig o'Balgownie. People could only cross by ferry or by fording the river. In Dyce there was a forked ford below Nether Kirkton about a mile west of where the Parkhill Bridge is situated. The old Banff road led down to the ford, which ran at an angle and was so clear it appeared to have been constructed from a plan. Part of the rough road, which starts at Greenburn, can be seen running through a farm near Dyce West Church, then it gets lost.

The bridge over the Don was built when the new road to Banff was made in 1851.

The present Parkhill Bridge was built at the same point as the old bridge and when the water level is low the support of the old bridge is visible.

Many years ago some mussel pearls were collected from the river here.

Before the railway line was built the path of the river was altered. The route of the River Don had been the old parish boundary. In the big floods of 1995 the Don broke down the retaining bank at the point of its old course. This bank was built up to protect the fields from flooding.

THE RIVER (unsubstantiated stories)

About 1750 one fine summer morning it was found that for about three miles below the church of Dyce, the bed of the river was entirely empty. Between 5am and 6am several people kept returning to the river to gather up the fish which lay sprawling on the bottom. No one actually saw how this drying up of the river happened and after about half an hour the water came down the river as usual. The only explanation given was that there had been an earthquake somewhere along the course of the river bed. A few people reported that they had felt an earth tremor.

Next to the Corn Mill is the Fae-me-well whirlpool. A horse and cart were swept down river and drowned in the pool that is apparently over 100ft deep.

The River Don was so low in summer 1942 near the Parkhill Bridge that people could have walked across. There were only small trickles of water running between large stones on the river bed.

THE TURNPIKE ROAD

The Inverurie turnpike road was formed about 1800.

The Old Toll House can be seen at the junction of the Newmachar Road.

The people who paid for the road charged tolls to pay for its building and upkeep. Every six miles or so small toll houses were built, some had curved walls for a better view of the road. A toll-house keeper lived there and collected money from travellers. A gate across the road prevented travellers galloping past without paying. Some gates were fitted with spikes on top to stop horses from leaping over. Amounts paid depended on the number of animals and on how many wheels were on the carriage.

'The Coming of Turnpikes to Aberdeenshire' by John Patrick

SCHOOLS

A small private school was opened at Caskieben but a school was required for the parish and in 1653 the first school was built at Pitmedden. It was set up by the Rev William Cheyne, minister of Dyce 1645-1675.

This was the beginning of education in the parish. Timber for the school cost £1 and 1/8 (8p) for a window and 'lum'. Pupils brought peats to heat the school. The first schoolmaster was Mr John Brown from Fintray who could perform marriages and baptisms for payment which added to his salary of 40 merks a year. Several parish schools followed at various sites.

Later a school was built at Overton near to Kirkhill and continued until the 1950s.The building is now a dwelling house.

Dyce Primary (the Old School) began as a school for infants and girls. Later it closed and re-opened in the 1890s as Dyce Village Public School. When it closed in 1974 the present Dyce Primary School, Gordon Terrace opened. Dyce Academy was built in 1980.

10. Overton School.

THE MELDRUM ROAD

In 1795 a Turnpike from Aberdeen to Banff was authorised but nothing was done until 1800 when a number of merchants and gentlemen proposed to make six miles of road from Old Meldrum towards Aberdeen. It was strange that the road building should begin at Meldrum and not on the route at the Aberdeen end but this was because that stretch would involve building a bridge over the Don at Dyce to replace the ford. This was expensive and it was not until 1802 that a group of subscribers got together to complete the road to Aberdeen.

These subscribers were determined to avoid losing money as often happened in road building and so they attached conditions to their subscriptions. First no one could be liable to pay more than he had originally promised. Secondly no more than half the subscription was to be spent on building the bridge. Finally no money was to be borrowed on the security of the Tolls.

In spite of the expense of Dyce Bridge (£2000) the road was under way. Contracts were awarded to Messrs Sutherland and Glass on 10th April 1802 when more than £3000 had been subscribed. By March 1803 when final promises had been made the total reached £5100.

The two ends of the road met in 1803. The road had three gates: one at Parkhill: one at Straloch and one at Old Meldrum. In addition the trust was entitled to half the takings at the Kittybrewster gate since it was assumed that half of the traffic on the road was bound for Dyce and Meldrum. The combined revenues had to maintain the road and provide interest on the £8000 capital. This was not easy but one subscriber Ramsay of Barra took an active interest in the day to day running of the road, inspecting the surface, and keeping an eye open for toll evasion. The rudeness of the turnpike men was notorious. They often attempted to cheat. Trustees were pleased when Ramsay reported any misdeeds but his keenness occasionally upset travellers.

To save money the bridge was made of wood that made it expensive to maintain and it was eventually replaced by a stone structure.

'The Coming of Turnpikes to Aberdeenshire' by John Patrick

KIRKHILL FOREST

In Kirkhill Forest can be found the Robber's Cave. (It is likely that the robber was a highwayman).

Also to be found is the Bishop's Stone.

A cross shape lies by the side of the Via Regia on the southern slope of the ridge above Bishopstone.

The cross is 64ft long and 49ft broad, its head points towards Bennachie and it is made from boulders and turf. It was intended to mark the part of hill belonging to the Bishop. The big flat stone is still in evidence. On it are cup markings and the letter M.

TAPPIES

On the summit of Tyrebagger Hill is a tower known as Caskieben Tappie.

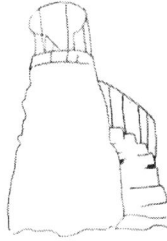

11. Caskieben Tappie.

Behind Pitmedden House on high ground is another tower with a flight of steps. It is the Pitmedden Tappie. The view tower inscription begins "Per Periculum Vivo erected on the fiftieth anniversary of Queen Victoria's visit to Aberdeen…"

12. Pitmedden Tappie.

BERRY PICKING

In years past people in Dyce went to the area round the Pitmedden Tappie to gather blaeberries for making jam. Wild raspberries were gathered in the area near the Old Church and brambles were gathered on the Hill of Dyce near Standingstones and Bogenjoss.

LOCHS

To the east of Parkhill House are three small lochs (there is some evidence of a fourth, the Ord Loch, in earlier times). The three lochs are Corby, Lily and Bishop; the last was formerly named Loch Goul. Corby loch is the largest and was mainly moss water bordered by marsh plants. Perch and trout were plentiful and were found to weigh on average half a pound.

Lily Loch is smaller. The Bishops of Aberdeen had, before the Chanonry was built, and for some time afterwards, their palace on an islet in Loch Goul. In early times the loch was much larger and was surrounded by woodland. The palace was reached by a drawbridge. Goval is the modern name for Goul. The islet also had a chapel connected to the Bishop's Palace. Although Bishop Hugh de Benham was a great and important man, his palace was small and more like a hermit's home. It is thought that the Bishop was burned to death within its walls in 1282. The loch is now known as Bishop's Loch.

Ruins remained and could be visited when the water was low but as the water of the loch is even lower now the islet is no longer surrounded by water. The foundations of the Bishop's Palace and the small attached chapel can still be seen and easily traced.

WILLIAM HAY

William Hay owned East Woodlands, Dyce, from the 1870s to the 1940s. He was a solicitor in Aberdeen. When he died aged in his 70s he gifted all his land, house and buildings to the Forestry Commission. Trees were planted and the land is now part of Kirkhill Forest. Standing in the forest is an upright stone roller with a name plate attached. It is surrounded by small posts and a chain. Mr Hay requested this to be erected to his memory.

THE RAILWAY

In 1887 the line opened between Aberdeen and Dyce. In Dyce a village was created on the edge of the moor. Major changes could take place when landowners encouraged building close to busy rail junctions. In 1865 feus were offered at the new village at Dyce Station. The station was advertised as having more passengers and goods traffic than any other station in the north.

The decision had been made to build the railway as far as possible on the bed of the Aberdeenshire Canal. The closure of the canal went ahead and railway building started speedily so as to minimize disruption of local trade. In fact the local contractor was so keen that the canal bank was cut and the canal emptied into the river while several were still completing their journeys. The break had to be made good and the canal refilled.

Parkhill Lodge

Parkhill Bridge

Dyce Church

Old Kirk Yard, Dyce

Old Kirkyard, Dyce: Symbol Stones

Quaker Mausoleum, Dyce

Liddel Monument

Bishop's Stone, Kirkhill Forest

Stone Circle, Dyce

Canal Mile Stone, Beidlestone Farm

Canal, Port Elphinstone

Canal Route at Dyce

Last Fly Boat, Canal at Port Elphinstone

Fountain, Station Road, Dyce

Toll House, Inverurie Road Junction

DYCE STATION

The station was situated at the junction for the Buchan and Formartine branch to Peterhead and Fraserburgh. When the railway was opened the area was bleak and was covered in moor and heather. It quickly became a flourishing village and the population kept on increasing. At the railway there were depots for stores. A creosote works was set up close by. As the station was a central point for the surrounding countryside slate yards, private woods and a manure factory were established there. The proprietor of the land was John Skene of Pitlurg and Parkhill. His home of Parkhill was less than two miles from the station.

RAILWAY STATIONS

To approach Pitmedden Station the train ran along, at a short distance, the west bank of the River Don. The opposite bank was dotted with several pretty country houses. These houses were summer homes of wealthy residents of Aberdeen. In the winter time they lived in the town. Above the station to the west, was the house of Pitmedden. It stood on a raised piece of ground and had a beautiful setting among the trees within the grounds. The owner was George Thompson merchant and shipowner.

Pitmedden Station had a brick-built signal box where the level crossing was controlled. Passengers could shelter at two small verandahs on the platform.

When the line to Huntly opened a station was put up on the farm of Nether Kirkton. This old station disappeared when the Buchan line opened in 1861 and the present station was built.

Dyce Station was much larger than it is now and it had more platforms and tracks. For some time there stood a tearoom in Station Road where passengers could enjoy refreshments. The village houses and shops were first built in the area near the station.

Some of the original houses and the Victorian signal box remain.

BLACKSMITHS

Dyce had at least two blacksmiths. The 'Smiddy' was on the site that was used by the car showroom and its neighbouring building in Pitmedden Road. A canal ring stone, where boats tied up, could be seen in front of the Smithy where the late Mr Gray removed it for preservation. Blacksmiths also worked at Station Road and at Locheye, on the left of the Parkhill to Bridge of Don road just after the entrance to Joss Quarry.

13. Dyce Smithy, Pitmedden Road.

THE PONDIES

Around the time of the station opening nearby lay two ponds separated by a line of trees and known as the Pondies. Here the village people enjoyed themselves in winter when the ponds were frozen. Two men kept the Pondies in trim and skaters came from Aberdeen to join in the skating and curling. This notice was displayed in an ironmonger's shop in Aberdeen.

DYCE POND OPEN FOR SKATING TODAY

RETURN FARE ABERDEEN TO DYCE 6d

3d ENTRY TO POND

On October 10th 1890 the *'Dyce Bazaar and Grand Ice Carnival'* programme was advertised in the *'Aberdeen Press'*:

Stalls	*Entertainment*
• *Antique and artistic furniture*	• *Refreshment stall*
• *Gems and ornaments*	• *Fortune reading and palmistry*
• *High class paintings*	• *Concert of classical music*

- *Spanish and Japanese pottery*
- *Game, poultry and dairy produce*
- *Chocolate and confectionery*
- *Flower stall*

- *Concert of popular music*
- *Shooting gallery*
- *Splendid tableaux vivants*

Dyce was chosen for the skating and curling rinks because it was a suitable distance from the city and because it was the centre of a very large working population who had comparatively little means of amusement and recreation.

The ponds were to be artificially lit and open until 10pm so that working people could enjoy them too.

> *At their opening, Sir Arthur Grant, Bart of Monymusk in his speech said that the ponds would be an attractive place for all classes of people to meet and about how the greatest duke could enjoy his game with the tinker or tailor out of the village. He also spoke of how skating was a good physical exercise for getting a girl's shoulders back as girls wouldn't skate well if they humped their backs like mice and went along with their noses on the ground.*
>
> *'Aberdeen Press'*

A total of £542 was raised at the bazaar.

Special trains were run to bring people from Aberdeen for the skating. The ponds were eventually drained.

DAISY COTTAGE

Probably the first house in Dyce Village was Daisy Cottage. It stood on the corner of Skene Place where now the bank stands. It is recorded that in 1908 Mr Sutherland, a carpenter, told how he built Daisy Cottage among the heather.

THE MAUSOLEUM

Near Cordyce School, beside the River Don, is the mausoleum built for the Quaker lairds of Dyce, the Skenes and the Gordons. The cemetery was built in 1689 and the surrounding wall heightened in 1837. Both families, the Skenes and their neighbours the Johnstons at Beidleston, were Quakers. The families intermarried, Anna Johnston to Alexander Skene Jnr.

14. Dyce Mausoleum.

LADY'S JOINTURE

The Lady's Jointure is a small field lying in a hollow west of the old UF Church of Dyce. Long ago the owner of Parkhill wanted to be separated from his wife therefore he promised her all the land that she could see from a point chosen by him. The gift turned out to be only half an acre due to the limited view. Therefore her jointure was certainly not a good deal.

NETHER FARBURN

Here is the meeting place of five successive forms of transport: The Old Banff packhorse road, the canal, the new Banff road, the railway, the aerodrome and now the new road.

MAINS OF KIRKHILL

An early name appears to have been Sleepiehillock.

PITMEDDEN

From 1857 the owners were George Thompson and his successors. The family was associated with the Aberdeen-Thompson Line of ships in the Australian trade.

A small colony of emus was a familiar sight to railway travellers.

The drive below the house is formed on the old canal line. There used to be an interesting bridge that carried the stream under the canal. The Pitmedden area used to be farm land except for a large chemical works, which was demolished, and a factory for manufacturing railway sleepers.

15. Canal Bridge at Pitmedden.

From Dyce follow the Pitmedden Road for half a mile and turn right over the Railway Bridge over the north line. Here on the right is a bunker built for defence during the Second World War. On the left is the sand quarry.

DYCE QUARRIES

At one time there was plenty of work in the area, in the mills and quarries. People came from the Highlands to find work but hours were long, conditions were poor and some of the work was seasonal. Quarry work was dangerous, people lost limbs and sight.

In the early 1900s many quarry workers began to emigrate to Red Granite in the USA hopeful of better conditions.

Stones from Dyce Quarries, now no longer used, were sent to London to be used in the building of London Bridge and the Customs House.

In war time conscientious objectors worked in the quarries without payment. Their living conditions were appalling, and the men there managed to produce a magazine called '*The Granite Echo*' to voice their concerns about the camp, which resulted in its closure.

ST MEDAN'S CHURCH

Near the Cothal Mills is the ruined church of St Medan and the churchyard where Lord Sempill of the Forbes-Sempill family is buried.

Until 1703 St Medan's was the parish church of Fintray.

SAINTS

St Fergus and St Medan were disciples of St Drostan who belonged to St Ninian's Mission at Whithorn.

Fetterangus, St Fergus and Dyce all owe their origin to St Fergus.

One story tells how when a great storm arose off Kirkton Head, Buchan and fishermen were in danger St Fergus took his bachuill (crosier) and cast it on the waves. The storm ended.

It is said that at the moment of his death St Fergus' spirit appeared in the church at St Fergus (previously named Lungley).

The embalmed arm of the saint was for long preserved in the Kirk of St Nicholas, Aberdeen.

St Medan founded four churches: Philorth near Fraserburgh, Auchmedan at Aberdour, Pitmedden at Udny and at Cothal near Fintray.

The ruined Kirk of St Medan stands on a beautiful bend of the river at Cothal. In the kirkyard are several sculptured stones. Legend has it that the people had a silver statue of St Medan. It was a special treasure to the Fintray parish and in times of drought was carried through the village. Rain always came soon afterwards.

At the time of the Reformation the statue was melted down and used to make a Communion Cup for the Reformed Kirk.

LOVELY BEND

The area at Cothal Mill is considered one of the beauty spots of the Don. The river curves at this point and when viewing from the high ground near the Old Kirkyard you can see the pool of the river below. The greenery of the trees partly hides the buildings of Goval-bank, Fae-me-well, and Cothal on the banks. In summer there is nowhere on the lower reaches of the Don which is nearly as attractive.

COTHAL MILL

Cothal Mill began in 1798 and used to be part of the Grandholm Works until it became unprofitable and was given up in the 1930s. Rags were taken by horse and cart from Aberdeen and elsewhere to the mills. There the rags were teased and made into flock, then they were taken to a factory in Aberdeen again by horse and cart. The flock was used for mattresses and cushions. Water from the River Don was used to wash the rags and to turn the water wheel.

There were three buildings and a small outhouse. One of the buildings has been knocked down, the other two are now houses and the outhouse is a shed or stable. The man who walked the horse six days a week got 19s 6d a week and had a family of twelve.

DYCE MILLS

In the old days Dyce Mills was called Femiewell (Fae-me-well) and although the name is now associated with the other side of the river it shows that in times past it was common for both sides of the river to have the same name. Sluices on the river allowed the mills to use water power in the milling of corn and barley.

THE HOLY CITY

For the first part of the 20th century Dyce was given the name 'The Holy City' because it had no public houses. Any liquid refreshment had to be taken at Stoneywood after a long walk along 'The Belties' which is now the Farburn Industrial Estate. In 1957 the Greentrees Bar was built.

WALKING

Local people used to enjoy going for their Sunday constitutional round Dyce's most popular walks, 'The Glen' and 'The Switcher'. The former started in Glen Road and ended roughly where Riverview Drive nears Stoneywood. It continued to be a popular strolling place until the early 1960s when houses were built there. The Switcher was the hilly road that skirted Dyce to the west via Pitmedden Road. It still exists in part but has been greatly changed by the Pitmedden Road Industrial Estate.

BAND

A popular entertainment for youngsters in the 1920s and 1930s was the Dyce Boys' Brigade Flute Band. Led by Mr Alex Winchester this band was renowned in the area.

DRAMA

Later, Dyce boasted a thriving dramatic society which entertained in all corners of the county with its productions of 'Jamie Fleemin' and 'The Cottar's Saturday Night'. It filled church halls everywhere in those days before television and even appeared in the Music Hall, Aberdeen.

SHOPPING

At the beginning of the century families sometimes existed on broth and plates of porridge which had been brewed up again and again for a whole week. A child might feel quite privileged to be given the top of his father's egg on a Sunday morning. A penny to buy a bag of bullseyes or a lucky tattie was a real treat.

Dyce had few shops in the early 20th century and the choice of food and other articles was limited and many people bought directly from the farm or grew their own food on small plots of land.

Just before the Second World War, when the airport opened in 1934 and Dyce became busier, the village had several shops situated mainly round the Station Road area. Mr Low's horse-drawn baker's van was a familiar sight. Along from the baker was Hector's shop where Dyce's first ice cream could be bought. 'Auld Winchester' had a general shop and Dick Hutcheon had one of Dyce's tailoring businesses off Station Road. Dyce also had a fruit shop, a shoemaker and a butcher. Life in Dyce was revolutionised by the arrival of Hughie Elrick's motor taxi and Yule's petrol pumps, but John Taylor still did good trade as a horse-carrier.

After the war, with the building of the large Berrywell housing estate, came the new Berrywell Stores and Dyce was well supplied with grocery shops.

ABERDEEN AIRPORT

The airport of Dyce was the brainchild of Gander Dower who started it in 1934-1935 with flights to Orkney in an aeroplane called a Rapide. In the early 1930s the airport was a private aerodrome.

In World War II fighter aircraft such as the Spitfire were based there.

THE WAR MEMORIAL

The War Memorial in Gordon Terrace was unveiled on Saturday September 3rd 1921. The names are inscribed of the people of Dyce who gave their lives in the war.

Dyce Roll of Honour.

The Great War (1914-1918)

John Ellison MacQueen
George Low
Andrew McKenzie Brown
Alex Booth
John Scott
Alex Mutch
Alexander Edmond Rae
John Ritchie
John Abel
James Anderson
Gordon Bathgate
Andrew Paterson Brown
Robert Currie
George Davidson
James Stephenson
William Edward
Alfred Fiddes
Frank Scott

James Rattray Scott
William Spence
George Taylor
James Taylor Gammack
John Low George
Alex Hector
James Kemp
Alexander E D Kynoch
Alexander Littlejohn
William Milne
Alexander Scott Murdoch
David Ingram Paul
George Robert Penny
Alfred James Philip
William Grant Pirie
Charles Raitt
Douglas Mackay Rattray
William Heard Reid

The Second World War (1939-1945)

A. J. Jenkins
R. L. Alexander
John Duguid
I. L. Ogilvie

William Pirie
Isabella Ross
John Reid

ARTIST

The painter, John Philip (Philip of Spain) was born in 1817 at 13 Skene Square, Aberdeen. His first job was as an errand boy to a tinsmith in Hutcheon Street, Aberdeen. He became an apprentice to a house painter and then studied painting in London and Spain.

He was regarded as a rich colourist and skilful composer. He became a respected painter of people and was regarded more as a portrait painter. Some important works by Philip are *'Baptism in Scotland'* and *'The Scotch Fair'* (believed to be Aikey Fair, Old Deer) which are in Aberdeen Art Gallery, *'Letter Writer of Saville'* and *'The Dying Contrabanista'* (both of which were in the possession of Queen Victoria and Prince Albert) and *'Miss Helen Allardyce'*.

John Philip was a relative of Mrs Allardyce, proprietrix of the Old Inn, Dyce, which stood beside the canal.

Mrs Allardyce was a widow with a large family and she expected all living at her house to obey her rules. Ten o'clock was closing time. Philip liked to visit The Old Inn in his boyhood days and he used to walk the six miles from Aberdeen. To a boy from the city Dyce was an interesting place. The house was full of young people. He could watch the coming and going of the canal boats and horses. He helped by looking after the animals and spent time exploring the banks of the Don. It was here that he painted one of his first portraits – 'Helen Allardyce', the daughter of Mrs Allardyce. 'Nelly' as she was called was his favourite and one day when he saw her dressed in a white dress for a dance he decided to paint her.

Also in his early days he painted the sign for The Old Inn. This signboard, lent by Mr Gordon, Parkhill, was on exhibition at the Bazaar and Ice Carnival held in the Music Hall, Aberdeen in 1890. One of the oldest residents of Dyce at the time, on being questioned about Philip replied – 'Oh, aye, fine dae I min o John. But, eh, figs! I didna like him ava, mony an awfu thrashin did he gae me!'

WRITER

James Macdonell also related to Mrs Allardyce was born in Dyce in 1842. He became one of the most brilliant leader-writers that the *'The Times'* has ever had.

MINISTER

'Cox of Dyce', The Rev Dr J T Cox (1865–1948) minister of Dyce from 1888 to 1936 was Principal Clerk to the General Assembly for eighteen years, and was author of *'Practice and Procedure in the Church of Scotland'*.

MATHEMATICIAN

Duncan Liddel (1561-1613) a mathematician who taught in universities abroad originated from the Pitmedden area. When he died Liddel left money to Marischal College and a monument in his memory was built on a knowe, in a field near the railway line, at Pitmedden. This monument was the first Granite monument in Scotland. A magnificent brass which originally covered Liddel's grave in the 'Toun's Kirk' of Aberdeen was preserved in the West Church of St Nicholas, Aberdeen.

ROBERT GORDON

Robert Gordon of Straloch, the famous geographer, was born at Kinmundy, in Newmachar in 1580. He was the first graduate of Marischal College and is known for his map of Scotland. His son James was the well known 'Parson of Rothiemay'. A grandson, Robert, was founder of Gordon's Hospital, Aberdeen and Robert Gordon's School.

LAWSONS

In 1934 Lawsons arrived at Dyce Bacon Factory. It began with a staff of about five men putting out about thirty bacon pigs per week. Lawsons at one point had a staff of about 700 and dealt with 4000 pigs and 400 cattle weekly. The factory was valuable as it was in the heart of the pig producing countryside. As it was near the Rowett Research Institute the scientists and the producers could work together for the benefit of both parties.

STREETS

Several street names remind us of the past in Dyce:

Fergus Place	St Fergus, bringer of Christianity
Southesk Place	The Countess of Southesk, landowner
Skene Place	The Skene family, landowners
Gordon Terrace	The Gordon Family, also landowners
Victoria Street	Queen Victoria
Gladstone Place	Prime Minister
Bishoploch Row	The Bishoploch
Gallowhill Terrace	The Gallowhill
Liddel Place	Duncan Liddel
Station Road	Still to be seen on the corner with Victoria Street is the ornate drinking fountain. It originally had a lamp on top. The lamp has been removed.

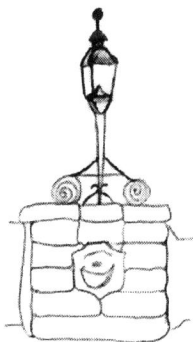

16. Well, Station Road.

STATISTICS

In the 1840s Dyce was described as a parish with good soil, thriving agriculture, rich woodland and healthy, long-lived people.

From '*The Statistical Account*' (1840s) prepared by Rev W Pirie Minister of the Parish, who later became Principal of Aberdeen University.

Population of the parish in **1755 1795 1861 1871**

383 352 585 945

The increase was mainly due to the houses built in the Gordon Terrace area near to the railway station.

Some details in that account were:

Rent of land	1 per acre	£2 10/-	a year to pasture a cow
Wages of workers	ploughman	£10	per annum
	women	£2 to £4	per annum
	carpenter or mason	1/3 to 1/6	per day
		(6p to 7 and a halfpenny)	
	blacksmith	£4 10/-	per annum

A monthly season ticket on the railway from Dyce to Aberdeen for a schoolboy in the 1920s was 5/7 (28p).

School fees were paid quarterly by pupils.

Salary of Head Master was £26 per annum.

School fees —			
	Reading	2/-	per quarter
	Reading and writing	2/6	"
	Reading, writing and arithmetic	3/-	"
	Mathematics	5/-	"
	Latin	4/-	"

POVERTY

The church was responsible for giving relief to the poor of the parish; people who do not have work or were unable to work. The money was paid quarterly and the same people qualified time and time again.

In 1840 poor people received about £3 1/11 a year. The Kirk got its 'Poor Fund' from the weekly collections that varied from 2/- on Communion Sunday to 4/- if a trainee minister was preaching.

Hospitals also relied on charity. Sometimes special collections were taken for special causes:

| 13th Oct 1822 | Aberdeen Infirmary | £3/ 11/6 |
| 29th Dec 1822 | The Lunatic Asylum | £1/ 3/- |

MORALITY

Nineteenth century moral codes were very strict, and kirk and elders were given responsibility for seeing that they were adhered to. Studies of Kirk Session records suggest that people who were thought to be guilty were taken before the Kirk Session to be 'chastised'. Sometimes they were fined. Some were persuaded to marry.

Elders were expected to be models of good behaviour and a Mr Farquhar was forced to resign because his son was considered immoral.

The whole population was expected to be church members. In Dyce only three people were noted as dissenters, one Roman Catholic and two Episcopalians who were elderly and only occasionally attended the established church.

PUNISHMENT

Christian Spence, wife of John Gray in Pitmedden, Dyce and James Gray, son of John Gray, who had been found guilty of setting fire to the cornyard of George Lessel in Pitmedden were sentenced to a restricted punishment owing to certain circumstances.

The court ordered that the two prisoners should be carried through the town in a cart with ropes around their necks and attended by the hangman. Then James Gray should be set free on condition he was banished from Scotland for life. Christian Spence would be imprisoned for ten weeks then keep the peace for three years or return to prison.

LOCAL STORIES

THE WITCHES

Most people would have put it down to bad luck. But John Wood, miller at the Mill of Fintray, knew who to blame for his broken mill wheel.

And when Isabell Straquhan or Skuddar was accused of witchcraft in 1770 John Wood was there to give evidence against her for having cast 'a devilish enchantment' on his wheel.

But worse, she was also accused of gathering the bones of dead bodies from the Kirk of Dyce and washing a certain William Symmer with water in which the bones had been dipped to cure him of sickness.

William's grandmother then disposed of the evidence of this ghastly remedy in the nearby Don 'and quhen they were cassin in the watter, the watter rummlit as if all the hills had fallen therein'.

We don't know poor William's fate but local legend has it that a witch was burned on the farm of Gallowhill.

Donald Walker, minister of Dyce in 1597 is described as a 'Complainer in a case of witch-craft.'

THE DWARVES OF DYCE

Dwarves of the Hill of Dyce told by a very old man to a young boy.

'D'ye ken there are caves in the Hill o' Dyce?'

'Caves', said the boy, 'No, I didna ken.'

'We'll,' he said, 'There are dwarves in the caves and they can be very bad tempered. Folk have gone into the caves and never come out again. Folk that see the doors of the caves should hurry by.

But despite this, the dwarves could repay a kindly act with a kindlier.

There was a crofter on the Hill o' Dyce and he found that someone was stealing his potatoes.

One night he watched and saw three dwarves digging potatoes with tiny forks. The old crofter left potatoes out at night for the dwarves to use in order to save them work.

When harvest time came, the old crofter was unwell and could not scythe his corn. But on looking out of his window one morning he found his corn cut and stooked and some days later he found in his cornyard seven of the finest ricks of corn between Dyce and Bennachie. Each one finished off with the likeness of a stem of tatties.'

'The dwarves do kingly turns laddie, but never trust them.'

MEMORIES

Mary Mackie, a resident of Dyce, was interviewed in 1971 and asked to recall memories of the Mill of Dyce where she was born. She told how the farm stood beside the river at the 'Crook o' Don' (the former Parish Church Manse).

To begin with the farm was a but and ben but was later enlarged.

She described the noise of the quarry machinery and how the quarries had extended in size to completely take in the Jinty Field, which was bordered on one side by the railway and the former canal and on the other three sides by trees. The beech trees beside the road were spared.

The kitchen of the farm had a blue-flagged floor, white scrubbed chairs, a wooden dease (couch), a meal girnal made from wood from the old Kirk of St Fergus, and an open fire over which was the 'swye'.

Also in the house were paintings by her uncle of views of the area.

Her father was keen on shooting, trout fishing and pearl fishing. Three Don pearls set in gold were in the house. The family had many a good meal from the rabbits, wood pigeons and trout caught.

Their nearest neighbour was the minister Rev J T Cox. Mary remembered carrying milk and cream to Dr Cox on her way to school at Overton. In those days people walked, cycled or went by pony and trap.

Boats were used to take people from the Fintray side to the Dyce - Pitmedden side of the river, especially for going to church. The McQueen family of Fae-me-well and the Crombie family of Goval Bank had boats on the Fintray side. Mary's family and John Cocker at Place of Goval had boats on the Dyce side.

On the Cothal side was a shop, 'Shoppie Willie'. It was low roofed and dark and the outside roof was the old style red tile. Mary used to row across to the shop and she told how that if she bought syrup, she brought her own jar that was filled from a large cask.

One year when the river was frozen over with thick ice at Goval Bank a wire was stretched from one bank to the other and held up by several posts. This was a safety measure for crossing.

INDEX

Allardyce, Mrs 27

Beidleston 9, 20

Belties 24

Bendauch Farm 3

Berrywell Stores 25

Binghill Castle 3

Bishop's Stone 14

Bogenjoss 8, 15

Brownie, Peter 6

Caskieben 12, 14

Cheyne, Rev William 12

Cothal 23

Cox, Rev J T 34

Croft of Pitdourie 4

Crombie 34

Crook o' Don 33

Dyce Bazaar 18

Dyce Free Church 5

Elrick, Hughie 25

Fae-me-well 11, 23, 34

Farburn Industrial Estate 24

Farquhar, Mr 31

Forests of Cordyce 1

Gariouch, Sir James De 1

Glubsgoval 4

Gordon 2, 4, 10, 20, 28

Goval 16, 34

Grandholm Works 23

Grant, Sir Arthur 19

Gray, James 32

Gray, Mr 18

Greenburn 11

Greentrees Bar 24

Hay, William 16

Hector 25

Hutcheon, Dick 25

Jinty Field 34

Johnstons of Cookston 1

Jollies Howe 8

Kirkhill Forest 14

Lawsons 28

Liddel, Duncan 28

Low, Mr 25
Macdonell, James 27
Mackie, Mary 33
Marcus Hill 1
McQueen 34
Mill of Dyce 33
Moss Fetach 7
Mountjoy Farm 3
Nether Kirkton 2, 7, 9, 17
Newhills 6
Old Inn House 9
Old Toll House 12
Overton 2, 12
Parkhill 4, 8
Philip, John 27
Pirie, Rev W 30
Pitdourie Well 4
References 37
Pitmedden 2, 7, 12, 15
Ririe, Johnnie 4
Robert the Bruce 1
Sempill 22
Shoppie Willie 34
Skene 4, 20
Skene, John 17
Sleepiehillock 20
Spence, Christian 32
St Drostan 22
St Fergus 5, 22
St Medan 22
Standingstones 1, 7, 15
Straquhan, Isabell 32
Sutherland, Mr 19
Switcher 24
Symmer, William 32
Taylor, John 25
Thompson, George 17, 21
Tyrebagger Ridge 1
Upper Kirkton 1, 2
Winchester 25
Winchester, Mr Alex 24
Woodlands Cottage 8
Yule 25

REFERENCES

Aberdeen Press   02.06.1868
                      10.10.1890
                      25.05.1937
                      15.04.1925 'John Philip'
Press and Journal   28.09.1934
                      06.11.1971
                      05.03.1975
Evening Express   04.03.1976
                      1980 'Only Yesterday'

Cox of Dyce – Rev J T Cox 1865-1948

Dyce Community Council – History of a Village by Valerie Moir

Dyce – Its History and Traditions by Cruickshank

Industrial History in Pictures – Scotland

Local Saints Deeside and Donside

Statistical Account 1840 by Rev Pirie

The Black Kalendar of Aberdeen by K Ferguson

The Canals of Scotland by Jean Lindsay

The Coming of Turnpikes by John Patrick

The Dyce Bazaar and Grand Ice Carnival 10.11.1980

The Great North of Scotland Railway by H A Vallance

The Old Inn by W J Jenkins